Contents

Foreword

It takes two to talk. So communicating with people who are not yet expert in English means both sides need to work at understanding each other. If you are already an expert, then you have a powerful set of resources which the other side does not have. And those with the most power are the ones that can take the most action to set things on course.

This excellent handbook gives a lot of straightforward practical advice about how we can adapt our language and interaction to make it more accessible.

It also encourages us to be reflective about our own talk and how we come across to the public. We take being able to talk and understand each other for granted, but it is important to be able to monitor our own style of speaking and writing.

Because English is the most widely used international language, many people have not had the experience of managing an extended conversation in a language they do not feel comfortable in. It is easy to underestimate how effortful and stressful this can be.

Monitoring and adapting our own way of speaking and writing can go a long way to making the communication easier to manage on both sides.

Lowering Language Barriers takes people on a journey into their own understanding of how talk works. It shows that even small changes in how we communicate may have large consequences for daily practices.

Its messages are clear and everyone working with the public should read it.

Celia Roberts
Professor Emerita in Sociolinguistics
Centre for Language, Discourse and Communication
King's College London

1 About this handbook

This handbook shows you how to adjust the way you speak and write so that you communicate effectively with people whose knowledge of English is more limited than yours.

Why read this handbook?
Skill in communicating effectively is essential when you interact with the public as part of your job. This means speaking or writing in ways that will help others understand us quickly, easily and accurately.

What does this handbook do?
It gives practical strategies and tips to help you communicate effectively with people who speak English as an additional language.

The booklet also helps you to communicate complicated or technical information to people who might not understand it because they lack the necessary expertise, experience or specific language.

Using the handbook

The booklet is divided into short self-contained sections. Read through them from beginning to the end - or dip in and out.

In **Sections 2, 3 and 4** we start with an explanation of the term 'English as an additional language'. We look at the impact of emotional barriers and how to start assessing a person's level of English.

Sections 5 and 6 explain the importance of becoming aware of how you use language and describe different styles of language you might use.

Sections 7 and 8 focus on spoken communication and what you can do to make it easier for people to understand.

Sections 9, 10 and 11 go into detail about how to choose words that are most easily understood and how to give clear explanations.

Section 12 focuses on the importance of slowing down your pace of talking and explains how to do it.

Section 13 and 14 focus on the importance of checking both what the other person understands and also your own understanding.

Section 15 gives suggestions on how to reinforce information by making it visual.

Section 16 gives practical tips on how to make your writing clear and easy to understand.

Section 17 highlights some of the ways in which culture can affect how people communicate and suggests ways of approaching cultural differences.

Section 18 considers the use of interpreters and Google Translate.

We finish with some thoughts on how you can help people who learn English – especially the words specific to your service.

Pause for thought
It is always useful to reflect on and talk about your own experiences. The handbook includes some reflective questions which will prompt this.

It can also be a tool to aid discussion with colleagues about communication at work:
- what are the challenges?
- what are you doing right?
- what could be improved?

2   English as an additional language

English as an additional language (EAL) – what does it mean?

We say that someone has English as an additional language when English is not the first or only language that the person grew up speaking or hearing at home. They may have learned English outside the home and they use it in addition to other languages.

What level of English do people with English as an additional language (EAL) have?

This really varies. The term itself says nothing about a person's level of ability in English. Some people with English as an additional language may speak and write English to a proficient level. Others may have only **basic** English.

In this handbook we are particularly thinking about the needs of people who are still learning to communicate in English.

How do skills vary?

There are four main language skills: speaking, listening, reading and writing. People may be stronger in one skill than another.

For example, some people may be confident or proficient in speaking English, but have only basic writing skills in English. Other people may find it easier to read information than to listen to information.

If possible, **ask** what the person finds easiest. This can help you decide what kind of help they may need. It might help them to have key information written down – as well as hearing it. Or, if they say they cannot write well, they may need help with filling in forms, for example.

Pause for thought

Can you remember learning a language?

Which did you find easier – speaking, reading, writing or understanding when listening? Why were some skills more difficult than others?

3 Assess the level of English

To adapt your speaking and writing so the other person can understand, you need to get some idea of their level of English.

How can you assess a person's level of English?
Start with simple, easy-to-understand questions:
> **What's your name?**
> **Where are you from?**
> **What language do you speak?**
> **How old are your children?**

Ask **open questions** (that is, questions which require more than a 'yes' or 'no' response).

How does the person respond?
Do they give very simple – or more complex – replies?
What words do they use?

If they seem confident in their understanding and responses to those simple questions, try using more complex language. Listen to how confident they are in responding.

Ask what they think of their English skills

Start with a reassuring compliment:

> **You speak good English...what**
> **about when an English person talks?**
> **How much can you understand?**
> **What kinds of things do you read in English?**
> **What about writing in English?**

Be aware

A person may **underestimate** their English language skills because they lack confidence.

Someone may be confident with everyday English, but not with less common language such as medical, legal or financial terms.

Other factors may affect the person

There may be other reasons why a person may not understand well, including stress, mental health conditions and learning disabilities.

4 Emotional barriers

Emotion can be a barrier to understanding. Feeling stressed, upset or anxious will affect a person's ability to communicate. They may not listen as well, or express themselves as clearly, as when they feel calm.

When a person cannot explain themselves as well as they could in their own language, they may start to feel frustrated and disempowered. This can, in turn, affect their ability to communicate confidently in that situation.

Not understanding makes things worse
Not understanding can make people feel stupid, embarrassed, excluded or vulnerable – particularly when they are already feeling stressed about other things, such as financial or health problems.

Sometimes, people will 'switch off' and stop listening if they feel uncomfortable because they cannot understand.

When you help a person to understand, they may be more likely to engage with you and your organisation or business in a positive way.

How can we use language to help reduce emotional barriers?

By speaking to someone in a way that is easy for them to understand, you help them to feel more in control. Feeling more in control helps them to be at ease. Being at ease helps a person to communicate better.

Pause for thought

Consider your own experience of not understanding.

When was the last time you found it difficult to understand some information?

How did it make you feel?

5 Be language aware

Being language aware means:
- **knowing** that some words and sentence structures are more difficult than others
- **noticing** your own and other people's style of English.

Why is it so important to be language aware?
The key to helping other people understand us is to speak and write in a way they will understand.

To adapt how we speak and write we need to be aware of **what** we say and **how** we say it.

Become more language aware
Start by **noticing** how others speak: colleagues, clients, people in public roles (for example, at the bank).

Listen to how they speak:
- what **words** do they use?
- how **fast** do they talk?
- how does this compare with other people?

After noticing others, start to **monitor** your own speaking and writing:
- how fast you talk
- when you speed up or slow down
- the words you use (and how complex they are)
- the amount of job specific or technical words you use.

Proof read carefully

When you write (for example, emails, letters or text for a website) look at how long your sentences are.

Notice the kind of words you use. Do you write the way you speak, or does your language change?

Pause for thought

How long did it take you to learn the specialized language where you work?

Do you already adjust how you speak and write?

Observe how you speak and write to different people such as managers, colleagues. strangers, friends and family. What kinds of English do you use?

When, why and how do you change the way you speak and write?

6 What styles of English do you use?

When we talk about lowering language barriers, it is helpful to think about different styles of English.

Jargon / organisational English
This style uses words and phrases specific to a sector or field of work, in other words jargon:

> **It's a paradigm shift which is intended to implement a new approach to service-user engagement with the centre.**

We often use jargon with work colleagues and can forget how difficult it may be for other people to understand the jargon.

Plain everyday English
This style avoids jargon and long or complex sentence structures in favour of straightforward everyday language:

> **It's a new way of thinking. The aim is to encourage people who use the service to get involved in the centre.**

Simplified English

This style is even more straightforward than plain English. It uses common words and short, simple sentences:

This is new. We hope it will help people to do things with us in the centre.

Which style is best to use?

Effective communicators will shift between the three styles. They adapt their style of speaking and writing to suit the audience.

Aim to use **plain English** most of the time, especially with the general public.

Simplified English is good to use with people who may find it difficult to understand plain English. This includes people who have a basic level of English as an additional language.

It may also help someone who finds it difficult to understand for other reasons, for example someone with learning difficulties.

7   Allow time for tuning-in

Everyone talks in a different way, for example accent, choice of words, volume.

Part of communication is tuning in to each other's way of talking – that is, **getting used** to the way the other person speaks.

This is especially important when:
- the other person is unfamiliar
- the accent is unfamiliar
- the topic is complicated and/or stressful.

How can you help the tuning in process?
Start with **small talk**, if possible. Chat about simple, safe things before you get down to business:

Have you been here before?
How did you get here today?

This gives you both time to tune in to each other's way of talking. It also gives you a chance to **assess** the person's level of English.

8 Prepare people for what they are going to hear

After you have allowed time to tune in and to assess the person's level of English, take a moment to explain to them:

- **what** you will talk about
- **why** you will be talking about it
- **how** you will be talking about it.

Try to be as specific as possible:

> **First, I will ask you questions about what happened last week. Then, I will tell you what the law says you can do. You can ask me questions whenever you want**
> is better than
> We'll sort out what needs to be done.

This scene-setting will greatly help the person to understand.

Be aware

People may not understand the **purpose** of some communication. For example, they may have **no experience** of an assessment, interview or review.

They may not understand what you expect of them or what they can expect of you.

Check if they understand **what** the meeting is about and **how** it normally proceeds. If they do not understand, explain the process.

9   Choose your words

Use words that are easy to understand.
Sections 9 –11 explain how to choose your words
carefully to make it easier for people to understand.

Did you know? English has a larger vocabulary than
many other languages. We have several words which
mean almost the same thing. People new to English
usually learn the **simpler** words first.

**Use clear, everyday English instead of formal words
and phrases**
> **before** (not prior to)
> **the law says** (not statutory requirement).

**Choose names that help people understand what a
group or job is about**
> **Group for fathers and male carers** is better than
> Saturdads
> **Advice Session** is better than Surgery.

**Avoid unnecessary professional or organizational
jargon**
> **This is important to us** not These are our core
> values
> **Check that you can have this** is better than confirm
> your eligibility.

Give the full name (avoid acronyms) when you first use it
Date of birth not DOB
Energy Performance Certificate not EPC

Avoid slang, idioms, and euphemisms
cut it fine, spend a penny, down there.

Be aware of multiple meanings
Many words in English have multiple meanings. For example, think of all the different meanings for the words surgery, notice, fine, coach.

Words with multiple meanings can be confusing for people learning English. You may need to explain the meaning or use another word.

Be consistent with the terms that you use
For example, if you are talking about **bacteria** and the other person understands that word, keep using that word. If you start using words such as germs and pathogens, you may confuse the listener.

10 Technical words

What do we mean by technical words?

These are words and terminology specific to a certain field of work or organisation, for example, finance, housing, medicine or the law.

Sometimes, when you are in a certain field of work, it is easy to forget that the terms you use may be unfamiliar to other people. If it is not necessary to use technical words, then they are best avoided.

What if you really have to use a technical word?

Sometimes there may be no alternative to a technical word. Or, you may want the other person to **learn** the word so that they can recognise it another time.

First use a simple word that gives them an idea of what you are talking about

> Before you move in you must sign a paper. This paper says what we must do and what you must do. We call it a Tenancy Agreement.

> I will send this information to someone who knows a lot about this problem. She is a speech therapist.

If you are referring to an event, describe what is going to happen in plain, simple language

> You will come to a room. There will be other people who know about your daughter, Sara. You will all talk about her. You can say what you want and what Sara needs. We call this a Review Meeting.

Give examples to help people understand

This is especially useful if you are talking about something abstract such as confidentiality, antisocial behaviour or safeguarding:

> All the people who work here must make sure that there is no danger for the children. For example we must make sure they cannot leave the room if there is no adult with them. This is called safeguarding.

Be aware

Some people with English as an additional language have a good understanding of technical words. What they may find difficult is understanding and using these terms in long or complicated sentences.

Listen to how people speak. Look at how they write. Notice the words they use and the complexity of their sentences. This will give you an idea of the language they can use comfortably.

Pause for thought

Think of when you started working for an organisation or business. How much new terminology did you have to learn?

11 Keep the message clear

Make your instructions clear and direct

Take away any unnecessary words (they tend to obstruct understanding):

> **Please tell us if you want to come** is better than We would be grateful if you could inform us should you wish to attend.

> **Speak to her as soon as possible** is better than I would suggest that you need to speak to her as soon as possible.

Visiting Order

1. The prisoner asks for a visit from you.

2. The prison sends you a Visiting Order.

3. You phone to make an appointment.

4. You come to visit.

   Bring the Visiting Order with you.

Top tip
If you want to sound **tentative**, use a simple word such as **maybe** or a simple phrase such as **If you want, you can...**

Use simple sentences
Start the sentence with **who** is doing the action:

> **I will send the form today. You need to return it this week** is better than The form, which will be sent out to you today, needs to be returned this week.

> **Someone from that office will contact you. They will give you a reference number. You need to keep that number safe** is better than You will be contacted by the office and given a reference number which needs to be kept safe.

Make your questions short and simple
Ask one questions at a time, rather than combining them in one sentence.

Repeat key words
Repeating key words also helps **reinforce** information and slows the pace of new words for the listener.

12 Speak slowly

Slow down your pace of talking

Why is this so important?

When you talk, you need to give the other person time to:

- **understand** the language
- **process** the meaning
- **formulate** their response.

People who are still learning English may be **translating** what you say into their own language.

They may also need more time to formulate their response. When you slow down, they get more time to do this.

Be aware

When you talk about **complex topics**, such as medical, legal or technical topics, people may need even more time to process what you are saying and respond. So, don't worry about long pauses!

How can you slow down your speaking?

Pause between chunks of words

First...we can talk about what you need...
I will write it on this paper...We call it an
assessment form...I will send the assessment
form to the office...Someone will telephone
you...This may be in one week.

Pause briefly between individual words

Short pauses between words will help to separate the the words. This will help people with basic English.

Very short pauses also help when you are talking on the phone:

> **You..need..to send us..your..application.. form.**

Say words slowly and clearly

This helps the listener to hear the words and then understand them.

Will talking slowly make you sound patronising?

This is a common concern but try not to worry. Usually the other person will appreciate that you are making the effort to help them understand.

Top tips

If you are worried about sounding patronising, ask the other person **Am I talking too slowly?**
Or say **Tell me if you want me to speak more quickly.**

Make sure you **don't over-emphasise** words by saying them too loudly or slowly. This will help you to avoid sounding patronising.

Give people time to respond to questions

Someone with basic English may think of a response in their own language first and then translate the response into English. Allow them time to respond.

Pause for thought

What makes people speed up their pace of talking?

Copyright @ Clare Hobart

13 Check they understand

It is not always easy to know if someone has understood us.

Often we **assume** that the other person has understood. We may think we can '**tell**' if they have understood. Unfortunately, we are often wrong.

Someone may honestly **think** they understand, but in fact they do not. Also, people **say** they understand when they **don't**.

There are many reasons why people say this. For example, they may not want to look stupid. It could be they are short of time or don't think the information is relevant.

To check understanding, we need to do **more** than just ask, Do you understand?

How can you check that the other person has understood?

Ask them to say what they have understood
This is really important. Can I check that I have explained it OK? What do you need to do when you get there?

Ask what they understand a word to mean
When I say the word, 'referral', what do you understand?

Remember, this may be difficult for people who can understand more than they can speak. So, another way to check their understanding is:

Get them to demonstrate their understanding
We talked about proof of identity. What proof of identity could you take?

What if someone doesn't understand?
It may be that the person understood **part**, but not all, of what you said. Maybe they didn't hear some of the words.

Give them another chance and try **repeating** what you said, maybe more slowly. If they still don't understand, you may need to rephrase what you said.

You can also ask them if they might understand better if you write down key points.

31

14 Check your own understanding

It may be difficult to understand someone who is still learning English, especially if they have basic level English and/or a strong accent.

It is really important to check what you think you have understood.

Repeat or paraphrase what you have heard

Can I check that I understand OK?
You say that you cannot come tomorrow.
Also, you say that you are going away for six weeks. Is that right?

What if you simply can't understand what the other person is saying?

- ask them to speak more slowly
- ask them if they can write down key words
- try not to get flustered about it.

People sometimes feel embarrassed when they have to ask someone to repeat themselves several times. Mostly, the other person will appreciate your efforts to understand.

Using a phrase like **Can you help me and say that again?** shows that you really want to help.

15 Make information visual

People may **understand** and **remember** information better if they see it in written or visual form as well as hearing it.

Write down key information and technical terms they need to know
This includes instructions, words, dates and numbers.

Remember: even if people can't understand it, they may want to take it away and show it to friends who can read English.

Other ways to make information visual
- **photographs** (for example, services they can use)
- **diagrams** (for example, showing what happens in the process of making an application or referral)
- **real examples** (such as a form they need or, if you are talking about dates, a calendar)
- **jargon buster or glossary** (for example, on your website).

Use digital technology to communicate in different ways
Video and audio recordings are a good way of presenting information and will help people who cannot easily read. They can be made available on websites or captured and carried on portable devices such as phones and laptops. For example, some medical consultants give patients an audio recording of their consultation.

Examples of visual information

These examples were used to support face-to-face explanations and conversations. Resources like these - even handwritten notes - can really help people **learn** key words as well as helping people **understand**.

English for Speakers of Other Languages (ESOL) – how to join (enrol)

1. We give you a time and date to meet with us.

2. We meet and you do an English test (assessment).
This will show us your level of English.

3. We tell you what classes are possible for you.
We tell you how much money you need to pay (fees).

4. You tell us if you want to join a class.

5. We give you a paper (enrolment form) .
You take this enrolment form to someone in Finance.
You pay Finance for the course.

6. Finance gives you a student identity pass.

Worcestershire
Regulatory Services
Supporting and protecting you

- Never store raw and cooked meats together in your fridge, use containers or different shelves
- Do not wash raw chicken
- Do not use dirty cloths on clean food surfaces
- Do not use newspapers to drain excess oil from poppadoms

7. Undercooking

- Thoroughly cook tandoori chicken, keema nan and kebab in the tandoori oven
- Thoroughly defrost chicken frozen blocks before cooking

Cross-contamination risk

Cross-contamination risk

Options

Interview

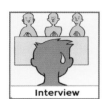

Paid work

Outdoor work

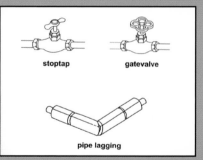

stoptap   **gatevalve**

pipe lagging

<u>Loan</u>

4·4% interest

You need

- current account more than 3 years

- Uk resident (live in Uk)

- 18 years or more

16 Make your writing clear

Many people find reading English a challenge. The way words are spelt, for example, can be confusing because written words don't always look like they sound. Think of 'rough', 'cough' and 'through'.

When we write English we often think we have to make it more formal. This can make it more difficult to read; but it need not. Good formal English is clear, straightforward and precise.

Ways to make your writing clear

Use short paragraphs and sentences
Try to ensure the **average** sentence length in your text is **15 – 20 words.**

Check the length of your sentences
Computers make it easy to count the number of words in any part of a word-processed text.
In **Microsoft Word** use the **readability function** to find the average length of sentences in a text. When you find a long sentence, look to where you could break it up with a full stop.

Keep to one idea in a sentence
Even if the ideas are related, keep them in separate sentences:

> **Please fill in all sections. Make sure you write your full name.**

Keep it short and simple.
Also, put the most important points first.

Use bullet points to break up text
Bullet points make writing clearer as they separate items of information. They also help draw the reader's attention to key items.

Use frequent headings
Headings help break up the density of text.
They also help the reader to know what the text is about and to scan the text for information.

Choose fonts carefully
- use a minimum font size of 12
- fonts such as Arial, Verdana, and Segoe UI are easy to read
- limit yourself to no more than three font sizes, two typefaces and two or three colours.

Avoid writing in BLOCK CAPITALS
Lower-case letters are easier to read because they have more distinctive shapes than upper-case (capital) letters.

Use **bold font** to emphasise text. Or <u>underline</u> the words if you are writing by hand.

Write dates in full
2 March 2015 is clearer than **2/3/15**.

Do you agree?
Everyone, whatever their level of English or their level of education, prefers writing to be clear, well-structured and easy to follow.

37

17 Culture and communication

When we meet people, we often notice the way they communicate. We may then interpret how they communicate as indicating something about them, such as their attitude or state of mind.

We all have preferred ways of communicating and using language. Someone who communicates in a way that is unfamiliar - or different to how we communicate - may appear rude or aggressive, for example.

To make more accurate assessments of people, we need to be aware of our reactions to other people's communication. We need to question the assumptions we may make – and be open to the possibility of cultural differences in communication style.

Here are some ways in which culture affects communication.

Politeness
Norms about **how** and **when** you show politeness vary from culture to culture.

In the UK people tend to use please, thank you and sorry **more** than people in some other countries. Saying "please", "thank you" and "sorry" in the UK way may seem odd to people from those countries. They may be used to asking for things in a direct way in their own language, and they do it in English too.

Asking for things and giving instructions

In the UK we ask for things indirectly when we want to be polite:

> We may say This work isn't quite the way I wanted instead of Do it again.

People from other countries may be used to asking for things in a more direct way.
What sounds blunt or rude to us sounds straightforward and normal to them.

Talking over each other / interrupting

There are cultural differences and preferences in the way people take turns to speak. In some cultures, it is acceptable to overlap another person's speaking. In other cultures, this is rude.

Be aware

Some people may not have enough English to be able to express things in a polite way.

How should you respond to cultural differences?

Here are some suggestions:

- be aware of your own reactions
- question your interpretations of the other person's behaviour; consider other possible interpretations
- become more aware of differences in people's communication styles
- ask people from other cultures what cultural differences they have noticed in the UK
- show respect for cultural differences.

Pause for thought

How well do you know yourself and your own communication style?

For example:

- how loudly do you talk?
- do you tend to fill in the pauses or silences in a conversation?
- do you tend to say things in a direct – or an indirect - way?
- how do you think you come across to other people?

Which aspects of your behaviour and your communication are influenced by your culture?

Do you agree?

It can be difficult to know whether a person's behaviour is part of their **culture** or their **personality**.

18 Working with interpreters

There may be times when you will need to use an interpreter, for example:
- if someone has very limited English
- when you are explaining complex information, such as a legal document.

Often, interpreters have English as an additional language themselves. They may have a high level of English, but equally they may not. Either way, be aware of the language you use.

Try to be as clear as possible
If you need to use technical words, check that the translator understands what they mean.

Google Translate
https://translate.google.co.uk/

Google Translate can be useful, especially for single words and short sentences. It also has an audio function.

Be aware that there are many words, for example 'safeguarding', which may have no exact equivalent in some other languages.

Top tip
It is best to translate the sentence back into English so that you can check how accurate the translation is.

Final thought

We all have a role in helping people to learn English

The better a person is able to use the language of the country they live in, the better they are able to integrate, find work, access services and contribute to society.

Learning English takes time – and it takes practice.

A lot of that practice takes place **'in the wild'**, through day-to-day contact with English speakers, including talking to staff in organisations and businesses.

If you work directly with the public, you will have opportunities to help people learn the language. Particularly, you can help people understand and remember the words, names and terminology specific to your organisation.

By following the practical tips in this guide, you can personally help people who are new to English to learn the language. Especially, the language they need to access your services and engage with your organisation or business.